Isaac Newton

Tony Allan

Heinemann
LIBRARY

H **www.heinemann.co.uk**
Visit our website to find out more information about **Heinemann Library** books.

To order:
☎ Phone 44 (0) 1865 888066
🖹 Send a fax to 44 (0) 1865 314091
🖥 Visit the Heinemann Bookshop at www.heinemann.co.uk to browse our catalogue and order online.

Produced by Monkey Puzzle Media Ltd,
Gissing's Farm, Fressingfield, Suffolk IP21 5SH, UK

First published in Great Britain by Heinemann Library,
Halley Court, Jordan Hill, Oxford OX2 8EJ,
a division of Reed Educational and Professional Publishing Ltd.
Heinemann is a registered trademark of Reed Educational and Professional Publishing Ltd.

OXFORD MELBOURNE AUCKLAND
JOHANNESBURG BLANTYRE GABORONE
IBADAN PORTSMOUTH (NH) USA CHICAGO

Designed by Katrina ffiske
Illustrated by Michael Posen
Originated by Ambassador Litho Ltd
Printed in Hong Kong

ISBN 0 431 10476 X
05 04 03 02 01
10 9 8 7 6 5 4 3 2 1

British Library Cataloguing in Publication Data
Allan, Tony, 1946-
 Isaac Newton. - (Groundbreakers)
 1.Newton, Sir Isaac, 1642-1727 - Juvenile literature 2.Scientists - Great Britain - Biography
 I.Title
 509.2

Acknowledgements
The publishers would like to thank the following for permission to reproduce photographs: AKG London 10, 13/Erich Lessing, 17/Erich Lessing, 23/Erich Lessing, 24, 30, 33; Art Archive 7/Private Collection, 27/Royal Society/Eileen Terry; Bridgeman Art Library 6/Lincolnshire County Council, Usher Gallery, Lincoln, UK, 25/Stapleton Collection, UK, 34/John Noott Galleries, Broadway, Worcestershire, UK, 37/Guildhall Library, Corporation of London, UK; Corbis 36/Jim Sugar Photography; Mary Evans Picture Library 11, 16, 18, 28, 29, 31, 35, 43; MPM Images 8, 12, 19, 41; By permission of the President and Council of the Royal Society 9, 21, 39; Science and Society Picture Library 4/Science Museum, 14/Science Museum, 20/Science Museum, 38/Science Museum; Science Photo Library 5/Volker Steger/Peter Arnold Inc, 22/Sheila Terry, 32, 40; Werner Forman Archive 42.

Cover photograph reproduced with the permission of AKG London.

Every effort has been made to contact copyright holders of any material reproduced in this book. Any omissions will be rectified in subsequent printings if notice is given to the publishers.

Any words appearing in the text in bold, **like this**, are explained in the glossary.

Contents

Piecing together the Universe

When Isaac Newton was born, in Lincolnshire, England, in 1642, the world was changing fast. During the **Middle Ages**, the Church had settled all questions about how nature worked. But by the 17th century the modern age was dawning. Great thinkers such as the Italian inventor and mathematician Galileo and the French **philosopher** Descartes had lead the way towards searching for proof about how the world really worked, and new discoveries were being made all the time. It was the beginning of the **Scientific Revolution** – and Newton was to become its champion.

This champion of modern science came from humble beginnings. The son of a farmer who could not even sign his own name, Newton did not come from a learned family. He had a lonely and unremarkable childhood. But it was as a student at Cambridge University that Newton's real talent was recognized. At the age of 26, he became the University's youngest-ever Professor of Mathematics.

Sir Isaac Newton aged 60. He was already a world-famous scientist when he posed for this portrait by Sir Godfrey Kneller in 1702, wearing a full-length wig.

Newton was born during a time of amazing scientific discovery. The previous 150 years had been a period of exploration, in which seafarers had pioneered the way to previously unknown lands: America, India, the East Indies and Japan. Then, at the turn of the 17th century, came the age of science. Technological breakthroughs unveiled new wonders: the telescope opened up the heavens, and soon after, the microscope revealed so far unseen miniature worlds.

Trial by mathematics

Before Newton's time, science had been a branch of **philosophy**. Students solved problems by talking them over, or by referring to the teachings of ancient Greek thinkers, such as Aristotle or Plato. These teachings had become accepted but there was no proof that they were correct. The world was buzzing with new ideas, but they did not fit together to make a whole. Newton linked together his ideas on movement, **gravity** and the way the Universe works to make sense out of the confusion. He made it his life's work to pick up the loose ends of the new science and tie them into a complete system – one that could be tested by experiments and backed up by mathematics.

Newton's method of careful observation and experimentation is the basis of science as we know it today. No wonder that people would come to see him as a new kind of hero – the explainer of the Universe.

An early microscope, designed by the Dutch inventor Antoni van Leeuwenhoek. To use it, people looked through a tiny round lens clamped between two brass plates. The specimen was placed on the pin at the top of the screw.

Early years

Woolsthorpe Manor in Lincolnshire, Isaac Newton's childhood home.

Isaac Newton was born on 25 December 1642 in Woolsthorpe, a small village in Lincolnshire. He never knew his father, a comfortably-off landowner, also called Isaac, who died three months before young Isaac was born.

Isaac was a weak and sickly baby, and he was not expected to live through the night. In fact he pulled through, but even so the outlook did not seem bright. He was the only child of a young widow with no one to help her run the family estate at Woolsthorpe Manor. When Isaac was 3 years old, his mother, Hannah, remarried. It was a decision that would affect Isaac for the rest of his life.

A lonely childhood

Hannah's new husband was a wealthy clergyman called Barnabas Smith. He was more than 30 years older than Hannah. He did not want to have his stepson living in his house. Barnabas insisted that Hannah should leave Isaac behind in Woolsthorpe when she went to live with him at his house in a neighbouring village. Hannah's parents moved to the farm to take care of Isaac, but that was little consolation. From being the sole focus of his mother's love and attention, Isaac now found himself seemingly abandoned. Hannah and Barnabas Smith had three children together, Mary, Benjamin and Hannah. Isaac had little to do with the other children. In the eight years for which her new marriage lasted, Isaac only saw his mother on visits.

A WARTIME CHILDHOOD

During Isaac's childhood, the **civil war** (1642–49) raged through England. **Royalist** supporters of King Charles I were fighting against **Parliamentarians** who wanted the king to rule only with Parliament's approval. After six years of war, the Parliamentarians won. There are no records of which side the Newton family supported. Although there was no fighting in or around Woolsthorpe itself, battles were fought as close as 100 kilometres (about 60 miles) away, and troops of soldiers must sometimes have passed through the village. It must have been an unsettling time for Isaac and his family.

A painting showing a battle during the civil war. Country life went on much as usual through the war years while the opposing armies clashed in battle.

The experience marked Isaac deeply. Throughout his life he was solitary and secretive, unwilling to trust other people. Isaac bitterly resented his mother and stepfather. He was always sensitive, and he seems never to have forgotten or forgiven the injury done him. Isaac's secrecy would come to cause him difficulties later in his life.

A growing mind

The village school in Woolsthorpe where young Isaac learned to read and write.

Very little is known about Isaac's early education, although he probably learned to read and write at the village school. In 1655, 12-year-old Isaac started at the secondary school in the town of Grantham, 10 kilometres (six miles) away. That was too far for Isaac to walk each day, so he went as a weekly boarder, staying at lodgings in the town. He was lucky to find a place in the home of the local **apothecary** (chemist), an educated man who owned books that Isaac was allowed to read. Isaac also got his first taste of chemistry from helping to mix medicines in the shop. He would continue to be fascinated by the subject throughout his life.

Making models

It may have been in Grantham that he found a book that was to change his life. It was called *The Mysteries of Nature and Art*, and it developed Isaac's understanding of mechanical devices, levers, pulleys and gears – knowledge that Isaac would find very helpful later. The book contained detailed instructions for making mechanical models. Isaac was good with his hands, and he threw himself into model-making with a passion.

Isaac made kites with firecrackers tied to their tails, sundials, a cart big enough to sit in with a crank to turn the wheels, and a windmill with working parts.

A quiet student

At school, Isaac would have been taught classical Latin and Greek, Bible studies and some English grammar. At first Isaac was a shy student, very much caught up in his own thoughts. But he made some friends when a local bully picked on him; Isaac challenged him to a fight and won. His schoolwork also improved, and he became head boy of the school. By the time Isaac was in his mid-teens, his teachers realized that he had the makings of a university scholar. But that was not what his mother had in mind for him. She needed Isaac to run the family estate. So at the age of 16 he was taken out of school and returned to Woolsthorpe to work on the farm.

The move was a disaster. Isaac had never shown any interest in farm work – his mind was on his studies and he often forgot his farm duties. When he was 18, Isaac must have been delighted when Hannah finally agreed to let him go back to school in Grantham to prepare for a university place.

Isaac Newton aged 12 in 1655, the year he left home to attend the King's School in Grantham.

A changing world

When Isaac left the farm in 1661 it was an exciting time to be starting a scientific career. The **civil war** was long over, and in 1660 the **monarchy** had been restored. Science was a new area of study, and in 1662 King Charles II gave official backing to the **Royal Society**, a scholarly club that was to become a centre of scientific knowledge in the years to come.

New developments

There was much for the society to consider. The **Scientific Revolution** was taking place and a flood of new discoveries in every area of knowledge was changing the way that people thought. In Italy, Galileo Galilei had built telescopes powerful enough to show sunspots and the moons circling the planet Jupiter. In Prague, Johannes Kepler had worked out precise mathematical formulae suggesting how planets move. There had been other breakthroughs, too. The thermometer and the **barometer** had been invented, while in maths **logarithms** had been devised (these are tables of figures that helped people to make complicated calculations). In medicine, the English doctor William Harvey had worked out how the heart pumps blood around the body.

Johannes Kepler analysed the motion of the planets before the invention of the telescope.

Testing theories

Behind all these breakthroughs was a change in the way people thought about the world. People such as Galileo and the French **philosopher** René Descartes had led the way in challenging accepted authority – not just the Church but the Greek and Roman writers, too. Instead, they said that scientific knowledge must be established by tests, experiments and mathematical proof. These were the ideas that stirred Isaac's imagination when he took his place at Cambridge University, and they were the foundations on which he would build his entire career.

In the years before Newton's birth, the Italian scientist Galileo Galilei had made ground-breaking discoveries using telescopes of his own making.

Ancient Greek thinkers such as Aristotle and Plato believed that the Earth was the centre of the Universe. They thought that the Moon and planets moved around the Earth in perfect circles, fixed for ever to spinning, transparent spheres of glass-like crystal. For nearly 2000 years, no one challenged these ideas. Then, around the year 1600, a Dutch spectacle maker called Hans Lippershey invented the spyglass, which Galileo later developed into the telescope. Soon, astronomers could see craters on the Moon, comets flashing through the skies and previously unknown moons circling other planets. The heavens were not perfect and unchanging after all – the Greek thinkers had got it wrong.

The young scholar

Cambridge was less than 100 kilometres (60 miles) from Woolsthorpe, but that was a three-day journey on horseback in Isaac's day. When Isaac arrived in June 1661, he found a dirty, crime-ridden town where muggings were common. The town had a population of about 8000 people, while Woolsthorpe was a village with just a few farms. Cambridge must have seemed an amazing place to someone like Isaac who had never before been far from home.

Cambridge was, with Oxford, one of only two universities in England at the time. Isaac's mother chose to send him as a '**subsizar**'. This meant that as well as studying, Isaac had to pay his way by waiting on tables and cleaning up after his tutor. Isaac's mother could have afforded to pay his keep, but perhaps, having only unwillingly allowed him go to university, she did not want her son giving himself airs.

Life at Cambridge

The result was that Isaac had a miserable first two years, with few friends. No doubt he felt humbled by his lowly position.

Trinity College at Cambridge University, where Newton enrolled as an 18-year-old student in 1661.

He threw himself into his studies and into religion; he even kept a journal in which he wrote down lists of his sins. But as time passed, life for Isaac improved. In his third year, he made friends with a fellow student called John Wickins, with whom he was to share rooms for more than 20 years. Like Isaac, Wickins had a passion for science, and they worked together on many experiments.

It was at Cambridge that Isaac discovered the new learning. At first he spent most of his time studying the Greek thinkers who still made up most of the official course of study. But in 1663 a change showed through in his notebooks, where he kept detailed accounts of his thoughts and findings in Latin, the accepted language of science at the time. While he respected the great classical philosophers, Isaac wanted proof. He listed his own ideas, based on his reading of new thinkers such as Francis Bacon, Galileo and Descartes, under a series of scientific headings – 'Of Attraction Magnetical', 'Of the Sun, Stars, Planets and Comets'.

Objects that once belonged to Newton, including a gyroscope and a pair of compasses, adorn his desk at Trinity College, Cambridge.

In Newton's words:

'Plato is a friend, Aristotle is a friend, but truth is the best friend of all.'

(From Newton's notebook, written in 1663)

In fact, Isaac was so interested in the new learning that he neglected his official studies. When he came to take his final exams, he did not do very well. He was awarded a degree, but not a good one. However, Isaac's passion for the new learning had caught the attention of some of the college staff. More importantly, Isaac himself had discovered what he wanted to do with his life. He had found his career – as a scientist.

Experiments with light

A scientist conducts an experiment with a prism. Prisms were the keys Newton used to unlock the secrets of light and colour.

In 1664, as a third-year Cambridge University student, Isaac did his first serious scientific research. He had bought a **prism**, a block of clear glass with angled sides, from a stall at the annual Stourbridge Fair, held just outside the town. Like countless people before him, Isaac enjoyed viewing the rainbow of different colours that the prism produced when he held it up to the light. But he was not content just to admire it, he wanted to understand what he was seeing.

With Wickins' help, Isaac covered over the windows of his college room so that only a pinpoint of light could be seen. Then he arranged the prism to cast the pattern of coloured bands – known as the '**spectrum**' – on the opposite wall. Using other prisms, he carried out a series of experiments on the Sun's rays.

Unpicking the rainbow

Isaac wanted to know why the light on the wall did not appear as a white disc, like the shape of the Sun, but instead appeared as a series of coloured bands. He quickly realized that it did so because sunlight, or white light, was made up of light rays of different colours. As they passed through the prism the rays were bent slightly, or **refracted**, by different amounts so that the separate colours could be seen.

Noting how the prism broke the Sun's rays into the colours of the spectrum, Isaac's next step was to work out if the separate colours could themselves be broken up. So he set up a second prism in such a way that only the red band passed through it. But this remained unvaryingly red, and each of the other colours in turn also stayed the same. The conclusion was obvious to Isaac: the white light of the Sun was a different kind of light from the rest, because it was a mixture of all of them.

ONGOING IMPACT   Seeing stars

Isaac's work on the spectrum has had an impact on the development of **spectroscopy**, which has proved vital in modern astronomy. By studying the spectra, or bands of colour, created by starlight, researchers can gather vital information about the temperature and chemical make-up of distant stars – and even about the speed at which they are moving and the strength of their magnetic field.

Isaac was fascinated by light and went on to make many more discoveries in the field that he called 'Opticks'. However, Isaac had been secretive ever since his lonely childhood. He never felt that he could trust anyone completely, so the world had to wait for 40 years before he published his discoveries on the subject.

A prism separates light into the colours of the spectrum.

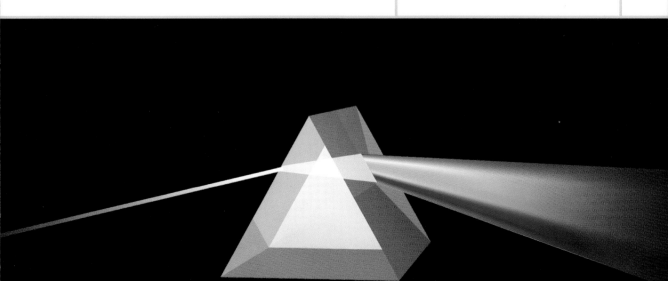

A marvellous year

When Isaac finished his university course in 1665, the **plague** was sweeping through London. It soon spread to Cambridge, too. Fearing an outbreak, the university authorities shut the colleges. Isaac had no choice but to return to Woolsthorpe and wait for the university to open again.

Undertakers' men collect the body of a plague victim who has fallen dead in a London street.

Back home, Isaac's mother had found other people to manage the farm, so his help was not needed. Instead, Isaac found himself with lots of ideas and plenty of time on his hands. He did not waste a moment. He stayed up all hours studying, writing and making calculations. Isaac had plenty to think about, because he already had the beginnings of many of his future discoveries in mind. There were his ideas about light to develop, and he was also doing groundbreaking work in the field of maths that would provide the testing-ground for all his later theories.

THE PLAGUE

The plague was carried from rats to humans by fleas. The disease had spread throughout Europe. It reached England in 1665, hitting London first, where at its height it struck down 10,000 people a week. It then spread out across the country, claiming the lives of almost 100,000 victims before gradually disappearing in the course of 1666.

An apple and a stroke of genius

But Isaac's stay at Woolsthorpe is perhaps best remembered for an incident he described to friends many years later. While sitting in the orchard one autumn day thinking about the motions of the Moon and planets, Isaac happened to see an apple fall from one of the trees. In a moment of inspiration it occurred to him that the force pulling the fruit to the ground might be the same one holding the planets in their courses, stopping them from flying off into deep space.

Some of Isaac Newton's belongings on display at Woolsthorpe Manor, which is now kept open to the public as a monument to the scientist.

What came to Isaac that day was no more than the germ of an idea – far from a fully-formed theory. It would take him many years to work out the details of what that moment of insight meant. But from that day on the seeds of the law of **gravity** were planted in his mind. That was the measure of his genius – to let an insignificant event in a country garden set in motion a chain of thought that would end up unlocking one of the fundamental laws of the Universe.

Discovering gravity

Newton watches an apple fall in the orchard at Woolsthorpe. Newton told friends that the sight helped trigger his discovery of the force of gravity.

For Isaac, the falling apple triggered the idea that the planet Earth exerts an invisible force on all objects. This force not only pulls an apple down to the surface, (and holds our feet there), it also reaches far into space and pulls on the Moon. The Moon's speed of movement means that it tries to go in a straight line, flying away from Earth into deep space. But the Earth exerts a force that continually tugs on the Moon to hold it back and make it move in a curve. It is almost as if the Earth is twirling the Moon around on a length of string. With these forces in balance, the Moon travels endlessly around the Earth.

The notion of gravity

The pulling force exerted by Earth is called **gravity**, or the gravitational force. Isaac quickly saw that gravity must be a feature of all objects, making them pull on, or attract, all other objects. Big objects have greater gravitational force than small ones. Also the gravitational force of an object fades rapidly with the distance from it. Your own body has a gravitational force, but this is too small for you to notice. The Earth's gravity is much stronger, pulling you down to the ground and keeping the Moon in orbit. The Sun is so huge that its massive gravity keeps all the planets travelling in orbit around it.

A space shuttle in orbit, circling the Earth at 28,000 kph (17,500 mph).

The law of gravitation

Isaac laboured on and off over the next 20 years on incredibly complicated calculations to prove his theory. The result was his law of universal gravitation. This linked together an object's weight, or mass, distance and gravitational force in one simple piece of maths, and it was one of science's greatest achievements. Newton's fundamental breakthrough made sense of the mysteries of planetary motion – and at last put to rest the ancient Greek vision of how the Universe worked.

A mathematical breakthrough

Gottfried von Leibniz, a brilliant German mathematician, challenged Newton's claim to have invented calculus.

To put his theories to the test, Isaac relied on mathematics. He had already realized that the accepted maths of the day was barely up to the task. But he also knew that he could count on the help of a secret weapon. Even though it was just two years since he had started to study mathematics seriously, Isaac had already taught himself all there was to know – and then had gone a step further. While still at Cambridge, before the plague struck, Isaac had begun to develop a new mathematical system of his own that he called fluxions. Today we know it as **calculus**.

ONGOING IMPACT Calculus

Newton's own system of maths, calculus, deals with situations where things continuously vary, for example, the speed of a car during a race. Using calculus you can work out how fast the car is going, and how much it is speeding up and slowing down, not over a minute, or even a second, but over an instant – in no time at all. In general science, it is probably the most widely used type of mathematics today.

Keeping the secret

Most young scholars would have wanted to tell the world about such an important discovery, but Isaac preferred to keep it a secret. He used calculus to carry out the hugely complicated mathematics that the study of **gravity** required. Yet when he came to publish his findings, in 1687, Newton chose to write out his evidence in conventional maths rather than reveal the way in which he had actually worked them out.

Returning to Cambridge

In 1667, after the threat of the plague had passed, Cambridge University reopened, and Isaac was able to return. There his work caught the eye of Isaac Barrow, Professor of Mathematics at Trinity **College**, who soon realized that Isaac had made important discoveries. To persuade him to make them public, Barrow showed Isaac a recently published work by a Danish mathematician who was also doing pioneering work on calculus.

Horrified to think that someone else might take the credit for his invention, Isaac agreed to let Barrow show a paper he had written to a few selected scholars, including the President of the **Royal Society** in London. The paper was enough to establish Isaac Newton's reputation as a rising talent. But still he would not agree to have the work published. Newton's secretiveness was to cause him problems later in life, when rival claims as to who had invented calculus would involve him in bitter arguments.

Arundel House was home to the Royal Society in 1667. Newton later helped to raise the money to buy a new building in Crane Court, London.

The young professor

By the time he circulated his paper on **calculus**, Isaac Newton had won a **Fellowship** at Trinity College, Cambridge. This allowed him to continue his research, and it also guaranteed him a tiny salary and a room in the college for life, in return for a few teaching duties.

On the strength of this success, Newton allowed himself one or two small luxuries and distractions – he had the rooms he shared with his friend John Wickins redecorated in his favourite colour, crimson, and even briefly took to playing bowls.

The Lucasian Professorship

Newton soon gave up such distractions, though, to get back to serious science. To get on in the academic world he needed the

support of older scholars. Isaac Barrow was an important ally. He was the first holder of the Lucasian Professorship of Mathematics – a new post created in 1664 and named after Henry Lucas, the college member who had put up the money for it. (The Lucasian Professorship still exists today, and the present holder is another famous scientist, the physicist Stephen Hawking.) Newton became Barrow's assistant. As well as doing his best to encourage Newton to publish his work, Barrow also paid him to check through his own lectures for publication.

Newton was a Cambridge professor when this engraving was made.

As a professor at Cambridge at the time, Newton did not have very much to do. He had to give 20 lectures a year, and to make himself available to students for a few hours each week. In fact he was not a good teacher, and most of his lectures were delivered to empty halls; often he cut them down from the hour allowed to 30 or even 15 minutes. Newton preferred to save his energies for his research, which soon won him such fame that the college authorities were happy to allow him to work as he wanted.

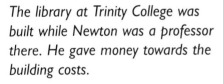

The library at Trinity College was built while Newton was a professor there. He gave money towards the building costs.

Barrow greatly admired Isaac Newton as a mathematician. So when in 1669 Barrow decided to leave Cambridge for London, he did not hesitate to recommend Newton as his successor. The university authorities took his advice, and on 29 October 1669 Newton was appointed the second Lucasian Professor. At the age of 26 he became the university's youngest-ever mathematics professor. It was quite a step for someone who had only scraped through his exams just four years earlier!

The sorcerer's apprentice

With his future at Cambridge guaranteed, Newton was free to follow his own interests. He soon developed a new passion – chemistry. At the time, chemistry was still closely linked to the age-old, semi-magical study of **alchemy**. Alchemists believed that, through experiments and meditation, they could eventually find the Philosopher's Stone, a magic substance that had the power to change inexpensive, or base, metals such as lead into gold. Another goal for alchemists was to find the Elixir of Life, a medicine that could keep people young forever.

Many people today are amazed that a genius like Isaac should have become involved in what is now seen as a fake science. But at the time it seemed there might be important secrets to be discovered; some alchemists had done pioneering work in chemistry in the course of their research. There was also a secret-society side to alchemy that may have appealed to Newton, who always saw himself as a seeker of hidden knowledge.

An alchemist at work. Alchemists believed that by studying, experimenting and living blameless lives, they could find the secret of turning base metals into gold.

The science of religion

Isaac Newton had other unusual interests. He had always been deeply religious, and felt certain that there were secret meanings to be found in the Bible. Newton's ideas almost got him into trouble with the Church, because he became convinced that Jesus had been created by God rather than being part of God's essence – an idea that the Church had long considered a **heresy**.

This could have lost Newton his place at Cambridge, for as a **Fellow** of Trinity College at the time he was supposed eventually to become a priest – something his unorthodox beliefs would not allow him to do. Fortunately, in 1675 he got permission not to fulfil the requirement from King Charles II, who was an enthusiastic follower of the new science.

Newton's Bible studies led him in some strange directions. He wrote books seeking to spell out God's plans for the future of the world from the words of the prophets and the Book of Revelation. He became convinced that there were hidden meanings in the layout of Solomon's temple in Jerusalem, as described in the Book of Ezekiel, and spent years trying to work out what they were. Although this research led nowhere, Newton continued to work on his theories right up to his death. Although they now seem to many people to have been a waste of time, to Newton they were just as important as his work on **gravity** or light.

An artist's impression of Solomon's Temple in Jerusalem. Newton sought hidden meanings in its plan.

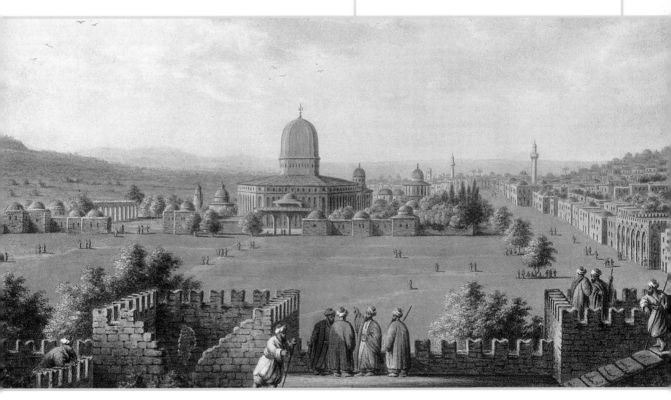

Newton's telescope

In a refracting telescope, light rays move in a single direction down the tube towards the viewer. In a reflector like the one Newton designed, the rays bounce back from a mirror at the end of the tube to a second mirror angled towards the eyepiece.

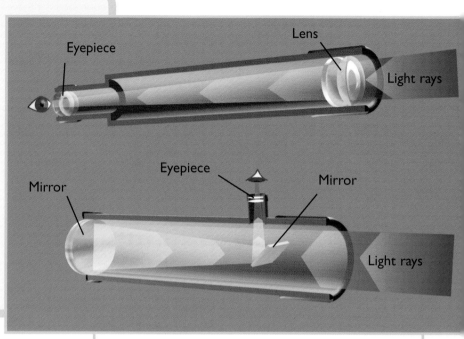

Diagrams of a refracting (above) and a reflecting (below) telescope. Newton's reflecting telescope not only gave a clear picture, but was also easy to use.

Newton had other things besides alchemy on his mind in the late 1660s. He had not lost his talent for making things, and now he put it to use as an inventor. Newton designed and built a new kind of telescope – one whose basic principle is still in use in most of the world's great **observatories** today.

Early telescopes

The first telescope had been made 60 years earlier in Holland by an instrument-maker called Hans Lippershey. He had hit upon the idea of placing lenses at both ends of a tube: one to collect light rays and focus them on to the other, an eyepiece that magnified them, at the far end. These first, **refracting** telescopes – so called because they bent, or 'refracted' the light – were crude devices. They were soon improved by Galileo and other astronomers, but they still made the images of stars fuzzy by surrounding them with a rainbow halo of colours.

Reflecting telescopes

Newton's solution was to use mirrors, which produced less distortion than lenses. His telescope had a curved, or **concave**, mirror at the back. This bounced the light rays forward again to a second, smaller mirror half-way up the tube. The second mirror in turn reflected the light to an eyepiece, placed at the side of the tube rather than at its end.

The idea of using mirrors instead of lenses was not new – it had been suggested six years earlier in a book called *Optica Promota* by a Scottish mathematician James Gregory – but no one had managed to make it work. Newton succeeded by doing everything himself. He produced his own design, made his own tools, and even ground his own mirrors and lenses. The results were even better than he could have imagined. The first reflecting telescope Isaac made magnified objects 40 times more than a much larger refracting telescope could manage.

This is the reflecting telescope that belonged to Newton.

The Royal Society

SERIOUS SCIENCE?

Although the Royal Society was already highly thought of when Newton joined, it was also involved with a lot of matters that would not now count as serious science. In those early days its members studiously listened to papers on such unlikely subjects as werewolves and ghostly spirits as well as on weighty questions of astronomy, physics and chemistry.

Many of Isaac Newton's theories were difficult for most people at the time to understand, but everyone could admire the reflecting telescope. It was Newton's ticket to success. When Isaac Barrow showed the new telescope to members of the **Royal Society** in London, in December 1671, it caused a sensation – King Charles II himself was given a personal demonstration. As for Newton, he was invited to join the Society – a great honour. The society's existing members (called **Fellows**) included such celebrities as the chemist Robert Boyle, Samuel Pepys, who was to write a famous diary of life in 1660s London, and Christopher Wren, who designed many buildings, including St Paul's Cathedral in London.

At the Society's meetings, papers describing new research were read and argued over. Soon after he became a Fellow, Newton sent a description of his work on light and colour to a meeting of the society. Although he was not there to read it in person, it was a great success.

Samuel Pepys, author of a famous diary of 17th-century London life, was a member of the Royal Society in Newton's day.

A meeting of the Royal Society. Newton joined in 1672, and later became its President in November 1703.

The price of fame

Still only 30 years old, Newton had by now made his name. As a Cambridge professor and a Fellow of the Royal Society, he was a rising star of English science. It had been a fantastic advance for a young man who was totally unknown on his return to university after the **plague** just five years earlier.

But Newton's new fame came at a price. By publishing his findings for other scientists to study, he was also forced to explain and defend them. Newton was a very private man who did not suffer fools gladly. He had little patience when other, less learned men questioned his results. At such times he would hurry back to Cambridge to lick his wounds, seeking the comfort of his alchemical research.

In Newton's words:

'I keep the subject constantly before me, till the first dawnings open slowly, by little and little, into the full and clear light.'

(Isaac Newton, when asked how he came by his discoveries)

Quarrels

Most of Newton's troubles at the **Royal Society** stemmed from one person: Robert Hooke. Like Newton, Hooke was a talented young scientist; but unlike Newton he was also very ambitious. Hooke was jealous of Isaac's success, and soon tried to belittle Newton's achievements.

Newton and Hooke first fell out over Newton's paper on light. Hooke had been appointed **Curator** of Experiments by the Society, responsible for putting new ideas to the test. But he had his own ideas about light and colour, and he dismissed Newton's theory without bothering to check it. Worse still, he claimed to have beaten Newton to the invention of the reflecting telescope, insisting that he had produced a similar instrument before the **plague** struck (though he had not kept it to prove his case).

This 17th-century engraving shows Robert Hooke carrying out an experiment on light using a pinhole camera.

ROBERT HOOKE

As well as being Newton's rival, Robert Hooke (1635–1703) was also one of the most talented scientists of his day. He did pioneering work in physics that helped pave the way for the invention of the steam engine. As an inventor, he devised improved versions of the microscope and the quadrant, an instrument used for pinpointing stars in the heavens. He was also an architect, who helped to draw up plans for rebuilding London after the Great Fire in 1666.

Rising anger

Newton was furious. He only published his discoveries unwillingly at the best of times. To have them challenged by someone he considered scientifically less than his equal seemed to confirm his worst fears about being misunderstood. Newton did not have the patience to argue his corner, so instead he returned to Cambridge and sulked, even threatening to quit the Royal Society altogether. The dispute was to simmer until Hooke's death in 1703.

The main effect of the quarrel was to drive Newton deeper into his alchemy studies at his laboratory in the gardens of Trinity College. He would stay up for much of the night, rarely going to bed before 3 a.m. while he worked on his alchemical experiments. There, one day in the winter of 1677, he suffered a tragic loss, when a candle fell over on his desk while he was out of the room, burning some irreplaceable manuscripts. Newton was devastated.

Newton received more bad news when his mother died in 1679. He returned to Woolsthorpe to sort out the estate. Scientifically, Isaac Newton fell silent. Many of his most important discoveries concerning **gravity** and motion remained unpublished – and so they might have continued, to the world's loss, if it had not been for the encouragement of a new friend, Edmund Halley.

This engraving shows Newton discovering the fire that destroyed many of his papers in 1677. Some versions of the story claim his dog started the fire, but in fact there is no evidence he kept a pet.

Newton's masterpiece

Newton's friend Edmund Halley was a fine scientist in his own right.

Edmund Halley was an astronomer who visited Cambridge to consult Newton on a problem involving planetary orbits. Halley was astonished to learn that Newton had already worked out the solution years before, but had never published his research. Realizing that Newton might have other important secrets to reveal, Halley spent months gently coaxing him to put all his findings down in print.

Principia

Finally Halley's encouragement paid off. Once he took up the challenge, Newton threw himself into the task of explaining his discoveries. He worked all hours on the manuscript, often going without meals and sometimes staying up through the night. The result, written in Latin, was his masterpiece. *Philosophiae Naturalis Principia Mathematica* (The Mathematical Principles of Natural Philosophy) was finally published at the **Royal Society's** expense in 1687. It was a book that was to change the course of science.

In Newton's words:

'In the preceding books I have laid down the principles of philosophy; principles not philosophical but mathematical. It remains that, from the same principles, I now demonstrate the frame of the system of the world.'

(From *Principia*)

The long-term importance of *Principia* only became clear in later years, when future generations put the ideas it contained to use. Over the years Newton's discoveries inspired inventors and engineers to devise machines and engines, clocks and measuring devices, eventually even trains and cars and spacecraft. Newton's ideas really worked; and many of the inventions that went to make up the modern world would never have seen the light of day without his insights.

Principia summed up all Newton's work in the fields of **gravity** and motion over the past 20 years. It described in detail not just how objects moved on Earth, but also how the planets moved through space. Most importantly, the book provided a mathematical framework that could be used to test Newton's ideas. Scientists soon realized that Newton had made a breakthrough in the study of motion.

The laws of motion

In the *Principia*, Newton spelled out his three laws of motion:

1. An object will stay at rest or will continue to move in a straight line at a constant speed unless some force acts on it.

2. When a force acts on a moving object, the object will accelerate in the direction of the force at a rate that depends on its mass and on the size of the force.

3. Every action has an equal and opposite **reaction**. (For example, when you let air out of the neck of a balloon, the air rushing backwards pushes the balloon forwards.)

PHILOSOPHIÆ

NATURALIS

PRINCIPIA

MATHEMATICA.

Autore *JS. NEWTON,* Trin. Coll. Cantab. Soc. Matheseos Professore *Lucasiano,* & Societatis Regalis Sodali.

IMPRIMATUR·
S. PEPYS, *Reg. Soc.* PRÆSES.
Julii 5. 1686.

LONDINI,
Jussu *Societatis Regiæ* ac Typis *Josephi Streater.* Prostant Venales apud *Sam. Smith* ad insignia Principis *Walliæ* in Cœmiterio D. *Pauli,* aliosq; nonnullos Bibliopolas. *Anno* MDCLXXXVII.

The title page of the first edition of Principia. *Newton wrote his masterpiece in Latin, the language of science in his day.*

The black years

Principia should have been the high point of Newton's life, but in fact it ushered in one of his worst periods. In his work, he threw himself back into his alchemist's studies, but they led nowhere. Any hopes he might have had of achieving breakthroughs in chemistry like those he had made in physics (what Newton still called natural philosophy) faded away. Newton was also lonely. He had never found it easy to make friends. His only close companion, John Wickins, moved out of Cambridge in 1683, leaving Isaac very much on his own.

This oil painting from 1688 by Henry Glindoni shows William of Orange and his advisers in a Council of War. Newton welcomed the arrival of William to become King of England. But his hopes of winning an official post from the new ruler were soon dashed.

Politics

With time on his hands, Newton got side-tracked into politics. In 1685 Newton's royal patron Charles II died and was replaced as king by his brother James II. James tried to force Cambridge University to offer degrees to Catholics, who at that time were denied them.

Newton, who was passionately anti-Catholic, helped organize opposition to the move. When James lost the throne in 1688 to the Protestant William of Orange, Newton turned out to have backed the winning side. For some months he had hopes of gaining an official position, but in fact nothing came of it.

When William of Orange became King of England, Newton, who had never before held a public post, briefly sat in Parliament as the appointed member for Cambridge University. He took little part in debates. It is said that the only time Isaac ever spoke was to ask for a window to be closed one day when he found himself sitting in a draught.

Depression

Convinced that his career was going nowhere, Newton sank into depression. The symptoms may have been made worse by the chemicals he breathed in regularly as he worked over his alchemist's furnaces. Recently researchers who have analysed samples of Newton's hair have shown that it contained high quantities of poisonous lead and mercury.

England's Parliament in the 17th century. Newton served twice as the Member for Cambridge University.

Eventually Newton snapped. In 1692 he suffered a nervous breakdown. Although he quickly recovered, the causes of his black mood did not go away. To fully regain his balance, he needed a new challenge, and in 1696 one came about in a most unexpected way.

Master of the Mint

Newton introduced ridged edges to coins to deter **counterfeiters**.

The challenge Newton had been waiting for finally came when he was least expecting it. Out of the blue, he was offered the job of **Warden** of the Royal Mint, the organization responsible for making England's currency. Newton was delighted, even though it meant putting his scientific research aside and leaving Cambridge, where he had lived for the past 35 years. In 1696, at the age of 53, Newton set off for London and a new life.

An important job

The job at the Mint was totally unlike anything Newton had done before, but it was an important one. The nation's money was under threat from forgers and 'clippers', who trimmed the edges off coins for the valuable metal they contained, gradually reducing their real value. To beat the clippers, the government had decided to call in all the nation's money and replace it with newly minted coins with stamped edges.

NEWTON'S NIECE

When Isaac made the move to London, his 17-year-old niece, Catherine Barton, came from Lincolnshire to serve as his housekeeper. She was the only woman, apart from his mother, who ever shared Newton's home. Catherine was a bright, attractive girl, and she got to know many famous people through her uncle, winning the admiration of such celebrities as the writer Jonathan Swift, famous for his book, _Gulliver's Travels_.

Workers at the Royal Mint producing coins in Newton's day.

The battle for the coinage

Newton took his new responsibilities very seriously. He found ways to increase the efficiency of the Mint, which was already working day and night to turn out the new money. He fiercely punished laziness and corruption among his staff. Newton even turned detective to track down forgers and clippers, often going to prisons or slums to seek them out and to cross-examine them. Many of those he helped to catch were later hanged.

Increasing responsibilities

It was a very different life from the academic calm of Cambridge, but Newton loved it. He was now a wealthy man, keeping a coach to travel in, and a staff of about six servants. He still loved the colour crimson, and had crimson draperies and bed hangings and a crimson settee at his home. Newton took on new responsibilities, too. In 1698, he re-entered Parliament, and in 1699 he was promoted to become Master of the Mint. Then in 1703, shortly after the death of his old enemy, Robert Hooke, he was elected President of the **Royal Society**. The black years were long gone. Now he was an important public figure, respected even by people who knew nothing about science.

Newton's last years

In his last years Newton found a fulfilment that he had long sought in vain. In 1704, a year after the death of his old enemy, Hooke, Newton published *Opticks*. Written in English to reach a wider audience, *Opticks* summed up Isaac's work on light over the past 40 years. The book was received with universal admiration, and it confirmed Isaac's position at the forefront of science. Across Europe he was by now seen as one of the great men of his time.

A great honour

As President of the **Royal Society**, Newton ruled almost like a dictator over the English scientific world, arranging for members who lost his favour to be expelled. He had a group of young followers who hung on his every word, regarding him as the guiding genius of the age. Newton was honoured outside scientific circles, too; in 1705 he was knighted to become Sir Isaac Newton, the first scientist ever to receive the honour.

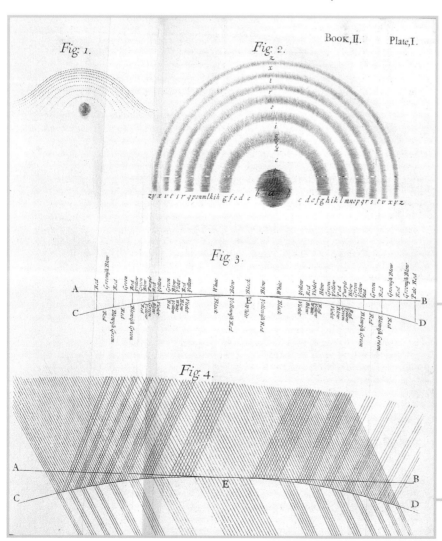

An illustration from Opticks, *Newton's last great work. Unlike the earlier* Principia, *it was written in English to attract a wider audience.*

Although he was a devout believer, Isaac Newton's religious views remained unusual. When a group of exiles from France known as the French Prophets began prophesying and having visions in public, rumour claimed that Isaac took an interest in their views. But he did nothing to help them when they were put on trial for disturbing the public order – even though one of the accused was a long-time friend.

Newton in old age. He lived to the age of 84, and was universally recognized as a great man.

Newton remained fiercely protective of his reputation. When the German scientist Gottfried Leibniz published his own version of **calculus**, Isaac bitterly accused him of stealing his ideas. He was unwilling to accept that any rival could have come up with the same answers without cheating.

After the publication of *Opticks*, Isaac did little new science, choosing to spend his time instead on ancient history and dating events in the Bible. He remained deeply religious, as he had been from his student days.

At last he had gained the recognition he had long felt was his due. When Newton died on 20 March 1727, at the age of 84, he was buried in Westminster Abbey, the resting-place of England's kings. Two dukes, three earls and the Lord Chancellor of England carried Newton's coffin to the grave – a mark of the enormous respect his work had earned him.

The new science

Isaac Newton was a pioneer of modern scientific methods, by which theories have to be put to the test to check that they really work. To prove his own ideas, he relied mainly on maths, which underpinned much of his research. That in turn was only possible because he had himself made revolutionary advances in the subject – progress that might have been even more influential if he had been less sensitive about revealing his secrets to the world at large.

The Grand Orrery

And all other Mathematical Instruments made and Sold by

BENJAᴺ: COLE,

at ÿ Royal Exchange or at his House in Ball Alley going out of George-Yard, into Lombard Street.

But the importance of Newton's work went beyond science alone. Before his day, the new discoveries made by the pioneers of the **Scientific Revolution** had challenged old notions without offering a new world view to put in their place. What Isaac offered was a whole new system to explain the working of the Universe – and one that could be understood by human reason.

An instrument maker advertises an orrery (a mechanical model of the Solar System). Demand for such devices surged in Newton's day.

The inner Solar System as we know it today. Newton's work was crucial in showing how the planets stay in their courses.

Newton's work on **gravity** had made him the first person in history to understand the way in which the Earth moves through space, and to explain the motions of the planets. Then he had gone on to show that, amazingly, the forces shifting the heavenly bodies were at work much closer to home, in the fall of an apple as well as in the Moon's orbit. This meant that the same principles applied on Earth and in space – a single theory to explain the whole Universe.

His discoveries may have been cosmic in scale, but they also had down-to-earth applications. His work was to inspire innumerable inventions that between them opened the way for the Industrial Revolution – and so for the modern world.

The effect on the way in which people saw the world was just as far-reaching. Isaac Newton's Universe seemed itself to work like a machine – one controlled by unbreakable rules. For Newton, a religious man, these laws had been established at the beginning of time by God – but God had framed them in a way that the human mind could understand. Reason, it seemed, ruled over all.

Newton's legacy

For 250 years Isaac Newton's model of the Universe reigned supreme, ushering in a new age of progress. His laws worked very well for describing how things move on Earth and in our own **Solar System** – the Universe Newton himself had known. Much of the modern world, from space rockets to satellite TV, could never have come into being without Newton's discoveries.

But with time knowledge moved on. In the centuries after Newton's death, new generations of scientists used better telescopes to learn more about outer space than Newton could ever have dreamed. Then, later still, improved microscopes uncovered another new world, this one of the very, very small – the world of atoms. In these areas, of unimaginably distant galaxies and of tiny atomic particles, new theories were needed to explain everything that came to light.

Newton's monument in Westminster Abbey, the resting-place of England's kings.

In Newton's words:

'I do not know what I may seem to the world, but, as to myself, I seem to have been only like a boy playing on the sea shore, and diverting myself in now and then finding a smoother pebble or a prettier shell than ordinary, whilst the great ocean of truth lay all undiscovered before me.'

(From Joseph Spence's *Anecdotes, Observations and Characters of Books and Men Collected from the Conversations of Mr Pope and Other Eminent Persons of His Time*, 1820)

Albert Einstein was the first person to seriously challenge Newton's view of how the Universe works, but he always acknowledged his debt to the work of his great predecessor.

More than 200 years after Newton, another genius, Albert Einstein, put his mind to explaining these fresh puzzles. The picture of the Universe he came up with proved very different from Newton's. From the 1920s, Einstein's view of a **relativistic** Universe, in which space could bend and mass could change, did not entirely replace Isaac's ideas but it did extend them. The Universe, it turned out, was more complicated than even Isaac Newton had imagined.

The many new pioneers of modern science could never have had their groundbreaking insights if Isaac Newton had not shown them the way. His ideas have never gone out of date; engineers working on high-technology projects still put his discoveries to use every day, and his laws are still taught to every would-be physicist.

Although Newton was in many ways a difficult man – a loner and a tireless worker who never found it easy to open himself up to other people – no man ever put his time to better use. By following the problems that obsessed him, he found something only a handful of people in history have ever discovered: a whole new way of explaining how the Universe works.

Timeline

1642   Isaac Newton born on 25 December at Woolsthorpe Manor, Lincolnshire. Isaac's father had died three months earlier.

1646   Hannah, his mother, remarries and leaves home. Newton's stepfather Barnabas Smith is the rector (clergyman) of a neighbouring village. Smith and Hannah are to have three children

1649   King Charles I is beheaded. England becomes a republic.

1654   Barnabas Smith dies. Isaac's mother returns to Woolsthorpe.

1655   Isaac enters grammar school in Grantham.

1660   The monarchy is restored. Charles II becomes King of England.

1661   Newton enters Trinity College, Cambridge, as an undergraduate.

1665   Graduates as a Bachelor of Arts. An epidemic of plague closes the Cambridge colleges, forcing him to return to Woolsthorpe.

1666   The 'marvellous year', in which Newton makes vital breakthroughs.

1667   Returns to Trinity College, and is elected a Fellow.

1669   Appointed Lucasian Professor of Mathematics.

1672   Presents his reflecting telescope to the Royal Society and is elected a Fellow of the Society.

1679   Death of Hannah, Newton's mother.

1682   Makes observations of what will later be known as Halley's Comet.

1684   Edmund Halley encourages Newton to publish his discoveries in the fields of gravity and motion.

1685   Death of Charles II. The pro-Catholic James II becomes king.

1687   Newton helps organize opposition to the offer of degrees to Catholics at Cambridge. Publication of his masterwork, the *Mathematical Principles of Natural Philosophy*, written in Latin.

1688   James II is driven out of England. William of Orange becomes king.

1689   Newton is elected to Parliament as the member for Cambridge University.

1692   Newton suffers a nervous breakdown.

1696   Moves to London to become Warden of the Mint.

1699   Appointed Master of the Mint on the death of the previous occupant.

1701   Elected to Parliament for the second time, holding the seat until 1705.

1703   Elected President of the Royal Society.

1704   Publication of *Opticks*, written in English to reach a wide audience.

1705   Knighted Sir Isaac Newton by Queen Anne.

1727   Isaac Newton dies on March 20 at the age of 84. He is given a state funeral and buried in London's Westminster Abbey.

Places to visit and further reading

Places to visit

Woolsthorpe Manor, Woolsthorpe-by-Colsterworth, Grantham. (Newton's boyhood home, now owned by the National Trust; has a permanent exhibition on Newton's life and work)

Grantham Museum (in the town where he went to school; has some exhibits about Newton)

London sites with Newton associations include: the Tower of London (where the Royal Mint was located); the Royal Observatory, Greenwich; the Science Museum, South Kensington; and Westminster Abbey, where he was buried and where an elaborate memorial now stands.

The Whipple Museum of the History of Science, Cambridge (has portraits and a replica of his reflecting telescope)

Further reading

Andersen, Margaret Jean: *Isaac Newton – The Greatest Scientist of All Time* (Great Minds of Science series) (Enslow Publishers, 1996)

Hooper, Meredith: *The Colour of Light – The Story of Isaac Newton* (Hodder Wayland, London, 1997)

Rankin, William: *Newton for Beginners* (Icon, Cambridge, 1994)

Robshaw, Brandon and Scholar, Rochelle: *Livewire Real Lives – Isaac Newton* (Hodder and Stoughton Educational, 2000)

Websites

www.newton.org.uk (easily the best place to start)

newton.gws.uky.edu (accesses the Isaac Newton Home Page, run from the University of Kentucky)

www.newton.cam.ac.uk (the website of the Isaac Newton Institute at Cambridge, with links to other Newton sites)

Glossary

alchemy an early form of chemistry, the main goal of which was to find the secret of turning ordinary metals into gold

apothecary old term for a chemist, in use up to the 19th century

barometer instrument for measuring air pressure

calculus advanced mathematical technique, separately developed by Newton and by Gottfried von Leibniz in Germany, that can be used to measure areas and volumes

civil war a war between citizens of the same country; in Britain, a war between Royalists and Parliamentarians fought from 1642 to 1649

concave curving inwards

college part of a university

counterfeiter forger; someone who produces fake money or other valuables

curator job title for someone who has responsibility for looking after things. So a museum curator is the administrative head of a museum

Fellow member of certain public bodies; at universities, the holder of a paid research post providing study facilities, usually in return for some teaching duties

gravity invisible force described by Newton that pulls objects towards the centre of heavenly bodies like the Sun, the Earth and the Moon

heresy going against the teachings of the Catholic Church

logarithms sequence of numbers, first worked out by the Scottish mathematician John Napier in 1614, that can be used to simplify the multiplication and division of large sums

Middle Ages period in European history between roughly AD 1000 and 1500 when the teachings of the Church dominated society and people's minds

monarchy form of government with a king or a queen ruling a country

MP Member of Parliament

observatories buildings with large, specialized telescopes set up to monitor the stars and planets

Parliamentarians supporters of Oliver Cromwell during the civil war. They fought against Royalists.

philosopher someone who seeks to explain the meaning of life

philosophy use of reason and argument to seek the truth and knowledge of reality

plague lethal infectious disease marked by the development of buboes or swellings, typically in the armpit or groin

prism transparent object, typically with rectangular sides and triangular ends, that breaks up light into the colours of the spectrum

reaction in Newton's theory, the equal and opposite force acting on an object when it exerts force on another object

refract bend

relativistic related to relativity (see below)

relativity concept developed by Albert Einstein to describe what happens to objects when they are travelling very fast, at or near the speed of light

Royalists supporters of the king during the civil war. They were fighting to keep the monarchy in Britain.

Royal Society club set up in London in 1662 to promote research into the sciences.

Scientific Revolution movement in the 16th and 17th centuries that produced new insights about how the world works by applying scientific techniques of observing, checking and experimenting

Solar System Sun and its associated planets

spectroscopy scientific method based on analysing the spectra given off by different light sources

spectrum colours into which white light breaks down when passed through a prism

subsizar in the 17th century, an undergraduate who had to earn his way through college by performing menial tasks

warden officer in charge of something

Index

alchemy 24, 28, 31, 34, 35
apothecaries 8
Aristotle 5, 11, 13
astronomy 11, 15, 26–7, 30, 32, 41

Bacon, Francis 13
barometers 10
Barrow, Isaac 21–2, 23, 28
Barton, Catherine 36
Bible 9, 24–5, 39
Boyle, Robert 28

calculus 20–2, 39
Cambridge University 5, 11–14, 16, 23
   mathematics 20–2
   politics 34
   professor 24–5, 28, 31
Charles I, King 7
Charles II, King 10, 28, 34
chemistry 8, 34
Civil War 7, 10
clippers 36–7
concave mirrors 27

Descartes, René 4, 11, 13, 27

Earth 18, 19, 33, 41
Elixir of Life 24
experimentation 5, 11

French Prophets 39

Galileo 4, 10, 13, 26, 27
gravity 5, 17–20, 19, 25
   disputes 31
   importance 41
   masterpiece 33
Gregory, James 27

Halley, Edmund 31, 32
Harvey, William 10
Hawking, Stephen 22
heresy 24
Hooke, Robert 27, 30–1, 37, 38

Industrial Revolution 41

James II, King 34–5
Jupiter 10

Kepler, Johannes 10

laws of motion 33
Leeuwenhoek, Antoni van 5
Leibniz, Gottfried von 20, 39
light 14–15, 16, 25, 38
   disputes 30
   Opticks 38
   Royal Society 28
Lippershey, Hans 11, 26
logarithms 10
Lucas, Henry 22
Lucasian Professorship 22–3

mathematics 5, 10, 11, 16
   gravity 19, 20
   legacy 40
medicine 10
Middle Ages 4
model-making 8–9
monarchy 10
Moon 11, 17, 18, 19, 41
motion 5, 17, 18, 19, 31, 33, 41

Newton, Isaac
   astronomy 26–7, 32–3, 42–3
   chemistry 24–5
   disputes 30–1
   early life 4–15
   education 8–9, 12–13
   gravity 18–19
   family 6–7, 9, 36
   mathematics 20–1
   professorship 22–3
   Royal Mint 36–7
   scientific career 16–17, 28–9, 34–5, 38–41

observation 5
observatories 26

Opticks 38, 39

Parliament 35, 37
Parliamentarians 7
Pepys, Samuel 28
Philosopher's Stone 24
philosophy 5, 10
physics 30, 34
plague 16, 20–1, 28, 30
planets 10–11, 13, 17–19, 32–3, 41
Plato 5, 11, 13
Principia 32–4
prisms 14–15

rainbows 14–15
reactions 33
reflecting telescopes 26–8, 30
refracting telescopes 26–7
refraction 14
Royal Mint 36–7
Royal Society 10, 21, 28–9
   disputes 31
   President 37, 38
   publications 32
Royalists 7

scientific method 5, 40
Scientific Revolution 4, 40–1
Smith, Barnabas 7
Smith, Hannah 6, 7, 9
Solomon's Temple 25
spectroscopy 15
spectrum 14–15
subsizars 12
sunspots 10
Swift, Jonathan 36

telescopes 26–8, 30

Wickins, John 13–14, 22, 34
William of Orange 34, 35
Woolsthorpe Manor 6–9, 12, 16–17
Wren, Christopher 28

48